CAPTAIN COOK

—Other titles in the Great Explorers of the World series—

COLUMBUS
Opening Up
the New World
ISBN-13: 978-1-59845-101-6

LEWIS AND CLARK
Exploring the
American West
ISBN-13: 978-1-59845-124-5

HENRY HUDSON
Discoverer of the Hudson River
ISBN-13: 978-1-59845-123-8

PIZARRO
Conqueror of the Mighty Incas
ISBN-13: 978-1-59845-128-3

HERNANDO DE SOTO
Spanish Conquistador
in the Americas
ISBN-13: 978-1-59845-104-7

VASCO DA GAMA
Discovering the
Sea Route to India
ISBN-13: 978-1-59845-127-6

CAPTAIN COOK

Great Explorers
of the World

Great
Explorer of
the Pacific

Stephen Feinstein

Enslow Publishers, Inc.
40 Industrial Road
Box 398
Berkeley Heights, NJ 07922
USA
http://www.enslow.com

Library of Congress Cataloging-in-Publication Data

Feinstein, Stephen.
  Captain Cook : great explorer of the Pacific / Stephen Feinstein.
    p. cm. — (Great explorers of the world)
  Summary: "Examines the life of Captain James Cook, a British explorer and scientist, including his
early life, his many Pacific voyages, and his death and legacy"—Provided by publisher.
  Includes bibliographical references and index.
  ISBN-13: 978-1-59845-102-3
  ISBN-10: 1-59845-102-2
  1. Cook, James, 1728-1779—Travel—Juvenile literature. 2. Explorers—Great Britain—
Biography—Juvenile literature. 3. Voyages around the world—Juvenile literature. 4. Oceania—
Discovery and exploration—Juvenile literature. I. Title.
  G420.C65F456 2010
  910.92—dc22
  [B]
                                        2009006503

Printed in the United States of America

092009 Lake Book Manufacturing, Inc., Melrose Park, IL

10 9 8 7 6 5 4 3 2 1

To Our Readers: We have done our best to make sure all Internet Addresses in this book were
active and appropriate when we went to press. However, the author and the publisher have no control over and assume no liability for the material available on those Internet sites or on other Web
sites they may link to. Any comments or suggestions can be sent by e-mail to comments@enslow.com
or to the address on the back cover.

♻ Enslow Publishers, Inc., is committed to printing our books on recycled paper. The paper in every
book contains 10% to 30% post-consumer waste (PCW). The cover board on the outside of each book
contains 100% PCW. Our goal is to do our part to help young people and the environment too!

Contents

Explorer Timeline   6

1 A Desperate Situation   8

2 The Call of the Sea 18

3 A Pacific Voyage 32

4 The Search for the
   Unknown Continent 60

5 The Fateful Pacific Expedition 78

6 A Captain's Legacy 96

Chapter Notes 103

Glossary. 107

Further Reading
   and Internet Addresses 109

Index 110

EXPLORER TIMELINE

1728—James Cook is born at Marton-in-Cleveland in Yorkshire, England, on October 27.

1736—Cook family moves to Great Ayton.

1745—Cook becomes an apprentice in a grocery and haberdashery shop in Staithes.

1746—Becomes merchant navy apprentice to John Walker in Whitby.

1747—Serves on the *Freelove,* a Whitby collier.

1748—Begins serving on the *Three Brothers.*

1752—Begins serving on the *Friendship;* is promoted to mate in charge of navigation.

1755—Joins the Royal Navy on June 17; sent to serve on HMS *Eagle.*

1757—Receives his master's warrant on June 29; joins HMS *Solebay* and then HMS *Pembroke* as master.

1757 –1762—Serves on the *Pembroke* in war against the French in Canada; surveys and maps Gaspé Peninsula, St. Lawrence River; serves on HMS *Northumberland;* begins survey of coast of Newfoundland.

1762—Marries Elizabeth Batts on December 21, 1762.

1763 –1766—Continues surveying and mapping the coast of Newfoundland; serves on HMS *Antelope* and HMS *Tweed;* in 1764 is given command of the *Grenville.*

1768 –1771—Cook's first Pacific voyage; Cook given command of the *Endeavour,* which sets sail on August 26, 1768.

1769—*June 3,* Sails to Tahiti to observe transit of Venus.

—Maps New Zealand and east coast of Australia.

1770—*June 11,* The *Endeavour* gets stuck on coral reef in the Great Barrier Reef.

1771—*July 13,* The *Endeavour* returns to England.

1772 –1775—Cook's second Pacific voyage; given command of HMS *Resolution;* departs on July 13, 1772, in search of the Great Southern Continent.

1773—*January 17,* Crosses Antarctic Circle.

—Stops at New Zealand, Tahiti, and the Friendly Islands (now the Tonga Islands).

1774—*January 26,* Cook crosses Antarctic Circle again.

—*March 11,* Arrives at Easter Island.

—Cook also visits the Marquesas Islands, the New Hebrides (present-day Vanuatu), and New Caledonia.

1775—*July 29,* Returns to England; provides evidence that the Great Southern Continent does not exist.

—*August 9,* Cook is promoted to captain.

1776—*February 29,* Cook is elected a Fellow of the Royal Society.

1776—Cook's third Pacific voyage; Cook, in command of the
–1779 *Resolution* again, sets sail in search of the Northwest Passage on June 25, 1776.

1778—*January 18,* First sights the Sandwich Islands (the Hawaiian Islands); the *Resolution* drops anchor at Waimea, Kauai.

—*March 6,* Sights the Oregon coast.

—After sailing along the Alaska coast and the Aleutian Islands, Cook sails through the Bering Strait and crosses the Arctic Circle.

—*August 17,* The expedition is forced to turn back by a wall of ice; Cook sails back to the Hawaiian Islands for the winter, hoping to resume the search for the Northwest Passage the following year.

1779—*January 16,* The two ships drop anchor in Kealakekua Bay on the Big Island of Hawaii; Cook is greeted as a god by the Hawaiians.

—*February 4,* The expedition leaves Hawaii but returns in a few days after the *Resolution* is damaged in a storm.

—*February 14,* Cook is killed by the Hawaiians after he takes a chief hostage in order to retrieve a stolen boat and a pair of tongs.

Chapter 1

A Desperate Situation

Shortly before eleven o'clock at night, on June 11, 1770, a leadsman aboard the *Endeavour* called out a comfortable 17 fathoms (102 feet). The leadsman's job was to hurl a heavily weighted line overboard to determine how much water lay beneath the ship. Earlier, around sunset, shoals had appeared off the ship's port bow. Captain James Cook steered his ship away from the shoals. He pointed the *Endeavour* toward what he believed was the safety of the open sea. So far, everything seemed to be going well.

The *Endeavour* was sailing in uncharted waters along the eastern coast of Australia. Although Cook did not know it at the time, the ship was well inside the Great Barrier Reef. Cook and his crew were actually in great danger, as they sailed slowly through a potentially fatal maze of shoals. But the sea was calm, and it seemed to be a fine night for sailing. Cook noted in his journal that they had "the advantage of a fine breeze of wind and a clear moonlight night."[1]

The leadsman took continuous soundings to determine the water's depth as the ship sailed. At about eleven o'clock, he was about to cast his lead again. Suddenly, the *Endeavour* struck an underwater coral reef. In Cook's words: "Before the man at the lead could heave another cast, the ship struck and stuck fast."[2]

Joseph Banks, a scientist on the ship, described the gravity of the situation in his journal. He wrote:

> Scarce were we warm in our beds when we were called up with the alarming news of the ship being fast ashore upon a rock, which she in a few moments convinced us by beating very violently against the rocks. Our situation now became greatly alarming . . . we were little less than certain that we were upon sunken coral rocks, the most dreadful of all others on account of their sharp points and grinding quality, which cut through a ship's bottom almost immediately. . . .[3]

STRANDED ON A CORAL REEF

Captain James Cook and the crew of the *Endeavour* were stranded. The ship had run aground, and the bottom of the *Endeavour* had been damaged when it struck the coral reef. Torrents of water began gushing into the ship. To make matters worse, a heavy swell beyond the reef broke as it crossed the reef. This subjected the stranded ship

Captain James Cook's crew refitting the *Endeavour* off the coast of Australia in June 1770. While sailing these uncharted waters, Cook's ship ran aground on a coral reef.

to a constant pounding, threatening yet further damage.

Captain Cook came up on deck almost immediately after the *Endeavour* had struck the reef. The men on deck could hear the dreaded grinding sounds of the ship's bottom scraping the coral. Cook launched the longboats so that men could take soundings for deep water. The reef upon which the *Endeavour* was stuck was a few feet below the surface in some places, somewhat deeper in others. Cook had his men drop anchors from the longboats. They then tried to wrench the ship off the coral reef. But the *Endeavour* would not budge.

Cook knew that a storm could tear the ship off the reef, causing it to break apart. They had to find a way to get free of the reef without destroying the ship. Cook's next strategy was to lighten the ship's load as much as possible. Hopefully, this would make it easier for the tide to lift the *Endeavour* and float the ship off the reef. All night the men hauled massive weights on deck and heaved them over the rail into the sea. Six cannons went over the side, as did food and water casks, firewood, and iron and stone weights. The crew lightened *Endeavour*'s load by at least fifty tons. But the ship still stuck fast to the reef.

The *Endeavour* had struck the reef during high tide. As the tide went out, the ship tilted more and more. The next high tide came and went the following morning, but the *Endeavour* remained stuck fast. Cook knew that the night tides on this coast were higher than day tides. So *Endeavour*'s best chance of being lifted off the reef by the tide would come the following night.

But in the meantime, the *Endeavour* continued to take on more and more water. Cook had the crew take turns manning the ship's pumps. In spite of all their hard work, the men were unable to prevent the water from rising inside the ship. By the next night, water in the hold had risen to almost four feet. Cook realized the desperation of their situation. He wrote: "The leak gained upon

This is an aerial view of the Great Barrier Reef. Captain Cook and his crew had to work hard and fast to break the *Endeavour* free from the reef.

the Pumps considerably. This was an alarming and I may say terrible Circumstance and threatened immediate destruction to us as soon as the Ship was afloat."[4]

Captain Cook, now throwing caution to the wind, ordered the men to throw overboard anything that might have been overlooked. He was determined to lighten the load further to make sure that the ship could break free of the reef. But even if they could get the ship off the reef, this would not guarantee their survival. Indeed, once off the reef, more water could rush into the ship and cause it to sink like a stone. The coast of the mainland was twenty miles away. There were not enough lifeboats for all of the crew.

According to Joseph Banks:

If (as was probable) she should make more water when hauld off she must sink and we well knew that our boats were not capable of carrying us all ashore, so that some, probably the most of us, must be drownd: a better fate maybe than those would have who should get ashore without arms to defend themselves from the Indians or provide themselves with food, on a countrey where we had not the least to hope for subsistance . . . and had they even met with good usage from the natives and food to support them, debarrd from a hope of ever again seeing their native countrey or conversing with any but the most uncivilized savages perhaps in the world.[5]

As the tide rose, the ship righted itself. Water continued to rise in the ship's hold. The exhausted crew waited in fear, dreading a possible disastrous ending to their ordeal. In his journal Joseph Banks wrote: "The anziety in every bodys countenance was visible enough . . . fear of Death now stard us in the face; hopes we had none but of being able to keep the ship afloat till we could run her ashore on some part of the main where out of her materials we might build a vessel large enough to carry us to the East Indies."[6]

FREE AT LAST

At around 10 P.M., the high tide rolled in. As everyone on the *Endeavour* held their breath, the ship floated off the coral reef. The *Endeavour* had been a prisoner of the coral for twenty-three hours. Although the crew was exhausted, they continued pumping water out of the ship. By morning, there was noticeably less water in the hold. Cook had his men plug leaks in the ship's hull with parts of a heavy sail. The pressure of the water kept the temporary padding in place.

Captain Cook was proud of his men, who had worked so hard to save the *Endeavour*. He wrote: "In justice to the ship's company, I must say that no men ever behaved better than they have done on this occasion, animated by the behaviour of every gentleman on board, every man seem'd to

Captain James Cook

have a just sence of the Danger we were in, and exerted himself to the very utmost."[7]

Captain Cook sailed his damaged ship toward shore. A fierce gale sprang up, but the *Endeavour* sailed safely through the storm. Had the gale struck while the *Endeavour* was stranded on the reef, the ship would most likely have been destroyed. But the crew, happy to be alive, did not mind in the least the driving rain and wind.

During the afternoon of June 17, the *Endeavour* finally reached land. Cook had the ship moored alongside a steep beach on the south side of the bay. He named the river that flowed into the bay the *Endeavour* River. Today, the thriving port of Cooktown (in present-day Australia) occupies the site. At around 2 A.M., the tide was still high. Cook had the bow of the ship hauled ashore, with the stern still in the water. Repair work on the *Endeavour* began the next morning. Cook inspected the ship, noting that there had been extensive damage to planks and timbers.

Ironically, the coral that had almost destroyed the *Endeavour* actually saved the ship. Captain Cook had wondered why the *Endeavour* had not sunk immediately, once it was freed from the reef. Now he knew why. A large piece of coral was jammed into the biggest hole in the bottom of the ship. The chunk of coral had sealed the hole, preventing the water from rushing in.

Chapter 2

The Call of the Sea

James Cook was born on October 27, 1728, at Marton-in-Cleveland, a small village in north Yorkshire, England. His parents, James and Grace Cook, lived in a two-room thatched cottage. James Senior was a hardworking farm laborer from Scotland. When James was old enough, he and his older brother, John, helped their father at work in the fields. Sometimes they helped him dig ditches and trim hedges. James learned the value of hard work from his father.

The Cook family lived at Marton until James was eight. In 1736, the Cooks moved to the nearby north Yorkshire town of Great Ayton. There, James Senior took a job as foreman at Airey Holme Farm. His employer, Thomas Skottowe, Lord of the Manor of Ayton, paid for young James's schooling until the boy was twelve. James attended the Postgate School in Ayton. Although he was not a particularly outstanding student, James excelled in mathematics.

Those who knew him at the time noticed that James showed traits of leadership and stubbornness. On various occasions, James and the other village boys would go out in the evening looking for birds' nests. James would have a plan, and the others would follow him to a location of his choosing. But sometimes the others decided it was time to change the plan. James would stick to his original plan, even after having been deserted by his friends.

Throughout his childhood, James Cook was never very far from the sea. The sounds and smells of the sea and the sights of sailing ships most likely had a great influence on him. William R. Gray writes about how Cook must have developed a fascination with the sea during his years at Ayton:

> I can imagine the farm lad, his chores complete on a lazy summer evening, scampering up the hill, stretching out on its rugged top, and gazing out across the miles to the North Sea. Large ships might have been beating against the wind, moving in the slow graceful fashion that only sail can give. Perhaps a roak—a dense sea mist—might have crawled inland at dusk, bringing the thick, musty, irresistible smells of the sea.[1]

In the summer of 1745, James Cook left home to become an apprentice in a grocery shop and haberdashery in the tiny fishing village of Staithes. Thomas Skottowe had arranged the trial apprenticeship with his friend William Sanderson, the owner of the shop. But life behind a counter held little interest for Cook. He would often gaze out the window at the ships coming and going in the harbor. He would hear the tales of the fishermen as he walked along the water's edge.

Cook worked for about a year and a half behind the counter of Sanderson's shop. Finally, Sanderson realized that Cook was unsuited to shop work. In the autumn of 1746, he took Cook

Cook moved to Whitby, a North Sea port in England. This statue of Cook stands in Whitby today.

to the nearby town of Whitby, a bustling North Sea port. There he introduced Cook to John Walker, who, with his brother Henry, owned and operated a small fleet of ships plying coal along the English coast. John Walker agreed to take Cook on as his apprentice.

Merchant Navy Apprentice

Cook lived with the Walkers, a Quaker family, where he had his own room. He attended a school for merchant navy apprentices in Whitby. There he learned navigation and how to read a sea chart. He learned the use of shipboard equipment and other important concepts of seamanship, such as the meaning of longitude and latitude.

In February 1747, at the age of eighteen, James Cook sailed from the harbor of Whitby aboard the *Freelove*. Cook's new life on the sea had begun. The *Freelove* was a flat-bottomed, slow-moving, bulky cargo vessel called a collier, or a "cat." Such a ship was designed to carry several hundred tons of cargo. The *Freelove* would load up on coal in Newcastle and deliver it for sale in London.

The North Sea was notorious for its difficult sailing conditions. There were frequent gales and sudden shifts of wind. Many of the harbors along the east coast of England were difficult to approach. Sailors had to contend with racing tides and sandbanks. The *Freelove* was perfectly designed for sailing in bad weather and in shallow seas. An apprentice such as Cook could find no better circumstances in which to learn seamanship. From the beginning, he paid very careful attention to the handling of the ship. As Cook watched Captain John Jefferson at work, he learned the various commands. He was not afraid to ask questions when he needed an explanation.

The town and harbor of Whitby looked like this in the eighteenth century. Cook left the port of Whitby in February 1747 aboard the *Freelove*, his first expedition at sea.

Apprentices on merchant vessels were expected to work hard. Cook soon proved himself by working harder than any of the other apprentices on board. He was usually the first on deck and the first to climb up the rigging. Cook's trip aboard the *Freelove* lasted almost two months. Back in Whitby, Cook continued studying navigation, as well as algebra, trigonometry, and astronomy.

In early 1748, John Walker was preparing a new large cat, the *Three Brothers,* for the coal trade. Walker assigned Cook to serve on the new ship, again under the command of Captain John Jefferson. Over the next eighteen months, the *Three Brothers* carried cargoes of coal to London. It also worked for the government, transporting foreign mercenary troops and their horses from Flanders to Dublin and Liverpool. During this time, Cook continued to expand his seamanship knowledge and abilities.

After serving on the *Three Brothers,* Cook worked for several years aboard various trading ships in the Baltic Sea. By April 1750, he had completed his three-year apprenticeship in the merchant navy. Cook was now officially a "seaman." Cook had gained considerable knowledge of the North Sea, the Baltic Sea, the English Channel, and the Irish Sea.

In 1752, Cook served on the *Friendship.* After passing all his examinations, he was promoted to mate on the *Friendship,* in charge of navigation. By 1755, James Cook was confident of his abilities to manage a ship. John Walker thought so highly of Cook that he offered the young man a ship of his own—the *Friendship.* James Cook had certainly come a long way in a relatively short period of time. Indeed, for a Yorkshire farm lad to rise so swiftly through the ranks of the merchant navy was remarkable.

Imagine John Walker's disappointment when Cook turned down his offer. Yet Walker was not totally surprised. He had once observed that Cook "had always an ambition to go into the Navy."[2] Cook knew that if he continued to work for Walker, he would have a very promising future. His loyalty to Walker would be rewarded, and he would always be assured of work in Walker's merchant fleet.

James Cook was clearly an ambitious young man. But his dreams pointed in a different direction. He realized that he could become a wealthy man in the coal trade. But delivering cargoes of coal along the coast of England no longer held much excitement for him. Cook longed to venture out into the vast oceans of the world. He yearned to see the lands beyond the far horizon. Cook made a difficult decision. Commanding a ship of his own would have to wait for the time being.

He would volunteer for the Royal Navy, even if it meant starting out in the low rank of able seaman.

John Walker regretted losing such a capable young seaman as James Cook. But he respected Cook's decision and offered to help him in any way he could. Walker gave Cook a glowing letter of reference for the Royal Navy.

THE SEVEN YEARS' WAR

On June 17, 1755, James Cook joined the Royal Navy. He was assigned to HMS *Eagle,* a sixty-four-gun warship, as an able seaman. At the time, Britain and France were aggressively competing for overseas territories. Both nations were frantically rearming in preparation for war, which increasingly seemed inevitable. Indeed, active fighting was already reported in several places, especially in North America.

Joseph Hamar, the captain of the *Eagle,* complained that there were no true seamen among the new recruits sent to him. In such a situation, James Cook stood out like a diamond amid junk jewelry. Not surprisingly, within a month of joining, Cook was promoted to master's mate. Soon after, Joseph Hamar was replaced by Sir Hugh Palliser. Captain Palliser, a young gentleman from Yorkshire, was a brilliant seaman and tactician. He and Cook gained each other's lasting respect. Palliser became the first to recognize that Cook was no ordinary seaman, but a man of genius and destiny.

The Seven Years' War between Britain and France officially began in May 1756. It was the culmination of a long economic and military rivalry between the two nations. The *Eagle* was assigned to patrolling the English Channel and the coast of France. In late May 1757, the *Eagle* and another British ship, HMS *Medway,* fought a battle with a large French warship. The fifty-gun French ship, called *Duc d'Aquitaine,* was crippled and captured during the flight. According to Captain Palliser, "She returned fire [ran the *Eagle's* log]. We engaged about three-quarters of an hour at point-blank range. She then struck. The *Medway* then came up astern. We were employed getting prisoners onboard and securing our masts and rigging. We killed 50 men and wounded 30. Our casualties were 10 dead and 80 wounded."[3]

The *Eagle* was badly damaged. But the Lords of the Admiralty were pleased at the outcome of the battle. Although Cook did not play an important role in the battle, Palliser recommended Cook for a promotion to master. Cook passed a difficult written and oral examination and on June 29, 1757, received his master's warrant. Then, on his twenty-ninth birthday, James Cook joined HMS *Pembroke,* a sixty-four gun ship, as master. Cook's new ship, commanded by Captain John Simcoe,

patrolled the Bay of Biscay. The *Pembroke* then blockaded the coast of France for the next few months. Then on February 22, 1758, the *Pembroke* sailed for Canada.

To conquer French Canada, the British would have to gain control of the St. Lawrence River. And British ships would have to prevent supplies from France reaching the French colonists. So sea power would prove to be the decisive factor in winning the war. As the *Pembroke* slowly made its way across a stormy Atlantic, many of the crew became ill with scurvy. This disease is caused by a lack of vitamin C, which people normally get from fresh vegetables and fruit. When the *Pembroke* arrived in Halifax, twenty-six men had already died from scurvy. Many others had to be taken to the hospital.

The harbor at Halifax was crowded with warships. One day, Cook watched as a great fleet of 157 British warships sailed away. He was disappointed not to be included in the huge armada. But the *Pembroke* had to remain behind until enough of the surviving crew had regained their health.

Cook the Surveyor

The British fleet was headed toward Louisbourg at the mouth of the St. Lawrence River. Louisbourg would have to be taken before the British could sail up the St. Lawrence to Quebec, the capital of New France. The *Pembroke* finally left Halifax and was sailing up the coast of Nova Scotia when the battle of Louisbourg began. By the time the *Pembroke* reached Louisbourg, the French governor had surrendered.

The next day, Cook walked along a beach near Louisbourg. He met a surveyor named Samuel Holland, who was making a detailed plan of the harbor. Cook wanted to learn how to use Holland's portable plane table. Holland discussed techniques of mapping with Cook, and the two worked closely on charts. By November, Cook had completed a chart of the Gaspé Peninsula. Throughout the winter, Cook, Holland, and Simcoe developed a chart of the St. Lawrence River. They completed their work by the spring of 1759.

In May 1759, after the ice broke up on the St. Lawrence, the British fleet began moving upriver. The path was clear all the way to Île d'Orléans. There, the river entered a treacherous region of shifting shoals and mud banks known as the Traverse. The fleet successfully sailed through the Traverse after Cook had carefully taken soundings and charted the channel. Not one of the 168 ships was lost. On June 27, the fleet lay anchored in the St. Lawrence River at Quebec. The British ships were out of range of the French guns on the cliffs above the river.

Captain Cook

CAPTURING QUEBEC CITY

After three months of minor skirmishes and raids, General James Wolfe drew up a plan for capturing Quebec City. The *Pembroke* and other ships made a feint attack down-river. Meanwhile, under cover of darkness, Wolfe led five thousand men into position above Quebec to make a stealth attack on the enemy.

The next morning, the French commander, General Louis-Joseph de Montcalm, faced the British with a force of about ten thousand soldiers. Although they greatly outnumbered the British,

James Cook served aboard the *Pembroke* during the Seven Years' War between France and England. This engraving shows the British landing in Montreal, Canada, on September 8, 1760, where the British would eventually win the war.

30

the French troops were exhausted and hungry. During the battle, which involved furious hand-to-hand combat, both Wolfe and Montcalm were killed. At this point, the French gave up. In his journal, Cook described the British victory: "[T]he English army commanded by General Wolfe attacked the French under the command of General Montcalm in the field of Abraham behind Quebec and totally defeated them."[4]

Cook was now transferred to HMS *Northumberland*. There, he served as mate under the command of Admiral Alexander Colville. During the next three years, Cook continued charting the St. Lawrence River and then the coast of Newfoundland. The *Northumberland* returned to England in November 1762.

At this time, James Cook was anxious to get married before he was sent away to sea again. He rented a room in the small town of Shadwell, just east of London. There he met a young woman named Elizabeth Batts. After a brief courtship, the couple was married on December 21, 1762. Apparently Elizabeth was not troubled by the prospect of marriage to a man who would be away from home most of the time. In the coming years, James and Elizabeth would have six children.

Chapter 3

A Pacific Voyage

After completing his service on the *Northumberland,* James Cook had sent his charts to the Admiralty. Cook's work was the product of several years of careful surveying and mapmaking. His charts included maps of the St. Lawrence River and parts of the coasts of Nova Scotia and Newfoundland.

On December 30, 1762, Lord Colville sent a letter to the Lords of the Admiralty. In it, he expressed the highest praise for James Cook's great work and abilities. He wrote:

> On this occasion I beg to inform their Lordships that from my experience of Mr. Cook's genius and capacity, I think him well qualified for the work he has performed and for greater undertakings of the same kind. These draughts [drafts] being made under my own eye, I can venture to say they may be the means of directing many in the right way, but cannot mislead any.[1]

⊕ SURVEYING NEWFOUNDLAND

On April 5, 1763, little more than three months after his marriage, Cook received an assignment from the Admiralty. His job was to survey and chart the six-thousand-mile coastline of Newfoundland. This assignment would take several years to complete. In the course of carrying out the assignment, Cook would have to sail back and forth across the Atlantic. In effect, he would become a sort of transatlantic commuter.

Cook sailed to Newfoundland on HMS *Antelope*, under the command of Captain Thomas Graves. In Newfoundland, Cook conducted his surveys in two ways. Sometimes he worked aboard the ship just off shore, and sometimes he made his measurements and calculations on land. After working aboard the *Antelope*, Cook transferred to a smaller ship, HMS *Tweed*.

When Cook completed his first survey of Newfoundland, he returned to England. When he got home on November 29, 1763, his wife Elizabeth proudly introduced him to their seven-week-old son, also named James.

In 1764, Cook sailed across the Atlantic again to continue his survey of Newfoundland. This time he received command of a schooner called the *Grenville*. On August 6, 1764, Cook was working ashore when an unexplained accident occurred. According to an entry in the *Grenville's* log:

> 2 p.m. Came on board the cutter with the Master [James Cook] who unfortunately had a large powder horn blown up and burst in his hand, which

shattered it in a terrible manner. One of the people who stood hard by suffered greatly by the same accident. Having no surgeon on board bore away for Noddy Harbour where a French fishing ship lay. At 8 sent the boat in for the French surgeon. At 10 the boat returned with the surgeon.[2]

By August 26, Cook's right hand had healed enough for him to return to his surveying work. After completing the season's work, Cook sailed back to England. He returned home early in December, in time for the birth of his second son Nathaniel. Cook returned to Newfoundland in 1765 and then again in 1766. Both years he worked on the *Grenville.* In November 1766, Cook returned home from his final season in Newfoundland. He spent the next eighteen months perfecting his charts.

On August 5, 1766, while surveying the Burgeo Islands off the south coast of Newfoundland, Cook had observed an eclipse of the sun. He recorded this event in such accurate detail that astronomers of England's Royal Society were greatly impressed.

Meanwhile, the Lords of the Admiralty were very impressed with Cook's survey of Newfoundland. The Admiralty would eventually publish Cook's charts of the area. More than a century later, Rear Admiral Sir William Wharton did surveying work in the same part of Newfoundland.

According to Wharton, "The charts he [Cook] made during these years in the schooner Grenville were admirable. The best proof of their excellence is that they are not yet wholly superseded by the more detailed surveys of modern times. . . . Their accuracy is truly astonishing."[3]

THE ENDEAVOUR SETS SAIL

In April 1768, James Cook planned another summer in Newfoundland. But the Lords of the Admiralty had other plans for him. Before even asking if Cook was interested, the Admiralty and the Royal Society had chosen him to command a voyage of exploration in the Pacific Ocean.

The Admiralty had several reasons for launching such a voyage. The reason announced to the public was to send astronomers to the Pacific to observe the transit of Venus, which would happen on June 3, 1769. A transit of Venus occurs when Venus's path or orbit around the sun takes it directly between the earth and the sun. When this happens, Venus can be seen as a little black circle moving across the face of the sun. Accurate observations of the transit would enable astronomers to calculate more accurately the distance of Venus from the sun. If this could be achieved, then the distances of the other planets in the solar system could be worked out. It was also thought that this knowledge would make navigation safer.

The Royal Society was interested in expanding scientific knowledge and, as such, was especially interested in the voyage to the Pacific. But the Admiralty also had its own important, though secret, reasons for the voyage to the Pacific. After defeating France for control of North America, Britain was rapidly building its empire. Voyages of exploration could provide new lands for an expanding British Empire. Britain hoped to discover and gain control over islands in the Pacific region before France could claim these lands.

Most importantly, the Admiralty would give the voyage commander secret orders to find the Great Southern Continent. It was widely believed at the time that a large, unknown continent, *Terra Australis,* existed in the South Pacific. Various mapmakers had long drawn imaginary versions of such a continent on their charts.

An astronomer of the Royal Society named Alexander Dalrymple believed in the existence of the mysterious continent in the Pacific. Indeed, he wanted to lead the proposed voyage. But the Admiralty insisted that a navy man be in charge of the voyage. They knew of no better person for the job than James Cook. Time and again, he had proved his value as an outstanding seaman and navigator. He had already commanded a ship. Nobody could match Cook's ability to survey and chart unfamiliar coastlines. In addition, his observation and recording of the eclipse of the sun showed him to be a capable astronomer.

Once the Admiralty decided to send Cook to the Pacific, they provided a ship for the expedition. They chose a Whitby collier, the type of ship that Cook knew best. The *Endeavour* was strongly built to withstand the heaviest seas. It was exceptionally wide, almost thirty feet, and a little more than one hundred feet long. The ship was slow and had not been designed for naval combat. The *Endeavour* could carry about one hundred people and a huge amount of cargo.

On May 5, 1768, the Admiralty notified Cook of his appointment to command an expedition to the Pacific. Twenty days later, the Admiralty promoted Cook to the rank of first lieutenant in the Royal Navy. The Lords of the Admiralty had previously been reluctant to grant Cook a commission as an officer in the Royal Navy. They had long held the belief that only upper-class gentlemen should hold such positions. But Cook was the most qualified seaman to command the expedition. So despite Cook's humble background, he got the promotion.

For the next few months, Cook was busy assembling his crew and taking on provisions. Finally by August 26, 1768, all the preparations for the voyage were complete. The *Endeavour* set sail from the harbor at Plymouth. Cook described their departure from England in the ship's log:

"At 2 p.m. got under Sail and put to Sea, having on board 94 Persons, including Officers, Seamen, Gentlemen, and their Servants; near 18 Months' Provisions, 10 Carriage Guns, 12 Swivels, with good Store of Ammunition and Stores of all kinds."[4]

Among those on board the *Endeavour* were a number of men with interests in particular areas of science. These included Joseph Banks, Dr. Daniel Solander, and Charles Green. Cook referred to these men as "experimental gentlemen."[5] Twenty-five-year-old Joseph Banks, a wealthy member of the Royal Society, specialized in botany. Dr. Daniel Solander was a pupil of the famous Swedish botanist Carl Linnaeus. Charles Green was an astronomer from the Royal Society. Also on board were the artists Sydney Parkinson and Alexander Buchan. The botanists intended to study unfamiliar flora and fauna and collect specimens. The artists planned to make drawings and paintings of the plants and animals. They would also paint landscapes and depict the human inhabitants of new lands.

As the *Endeavour* set sail, Joseph Banks wrote in his journal that all the company "were in excellent health and spirits perfectly prepared (in Mind at least) to undergo with Chearfullness any fatigues or dangers that may occur in our intended Voyage."[6]

●Bound for Tahiti

The Royal Society had determined that Tahiti would be the best place from which to observe the transit of Venus. Samuel Wallis, an English explorer, had recently discovered the south Pacific island and named it after the king of England, "King George the Third's Island." Wallis returned to England on May 20, 1768, just fifteen days after Cook's appointment to command the *Endeavour*. In a letter, Wallis wrote, "We have discovered a large, fertile and extremely populous island in the south seas. The *Dolphin* came to an anchor in a safe, spacious and commodious harbour. . . . From the behaviour of the inhabitants, we had reason to believe she was the first and only ship they had ever seen."[7]

The *Endeavour* sailed south in the Atlantic along the coast of Europe. It reached the Portuguese island of Madeira, off the west coast of Africa, on September 12, 1768. The first leg of the voyage had been relatively uneventful. At Madeira, Cook took aboard a cargo of water, rum, fresh beef, fresh fruit, green vegetables, and onions. Upon leaving the island, the *Endeavour* headed west across the Atlantic toward South America.

The basic diet aboard the *Endeavour* consisted of salt pork and biscuits. But Cook had also brought along ten tons of sauerkraut. He was determined that none of his crew would become a victim of scurvy. Although the men were unfamiliar with sauerkraut and were hesitant to eat it, Cook enforced strict dietary regulations. Sauerkraut was made from cabbage, which contained some vitamin C. When two crew members refused to eat the sauerkraut, Cook had them flogged. The two men did eventually eat the

From left to right, Earl of Sandwich, Dr. John Hawkesworth, Captain Cook, Sir Joseph Banks, and Dr. Daniel Solander. Several scientists accompanied Cook on his first Pacific voyage, including Banks and Solander.

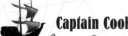

sauerkraut. Also, Cook stopped frequently during the journey to find fresh water and food that also contained vitamin C. As a result, by the time the *Endeavour* had been sailing for five months, there was no sign of scurvy aboard. In those days, crews typically became ill with scurvy after three months at sea.

CROSSING THE EQUATOR

On October 26, 1768, the *Endeavour* crossed the equator. Cook and the crew observed this event in the traditional manner. Any person aboard crossing the equator for the first time was dunked in the sea. According to Joseph Banks, "Sufficiently diverting it certainly was to see the different faces that were made on this occasion, some grinning and exulting in their hardiness whilst others were almost suffocated and came up ready enough to have compounded after the first or second [dunk,] had such proceeding been allowable."[8]

On November 13, 1768, the *Endeavour* arrived at Rio de Janeiro, on the east coast of South America. Banks and Solander went ashore and brought back an assortment of plant samples. After the *Endeavour* loaded up on fresh provisions, Cook sailed south along the coast.

On January 15, 1769, the *Endeavour* reached Tierra del Fuego, very near the southern tip of

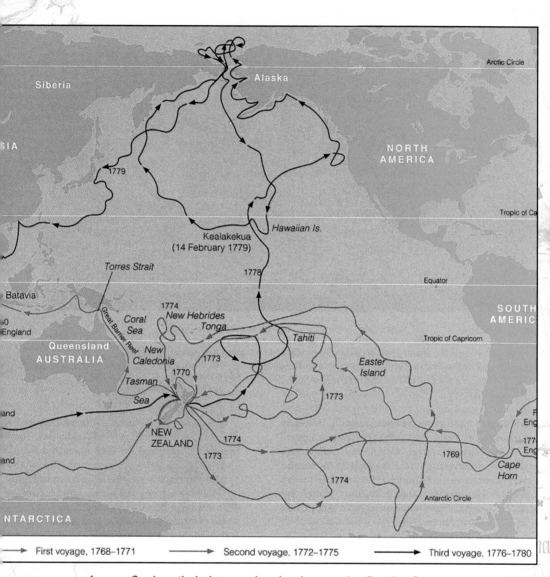

First voyage, 1768–1771   Second voyage, 1772–1775   Third voyage, 1776–1780

James Cook sailed thousands of miles on the Pacific Ocean during his life. This map shows the routes Cook used on his Pacific voyages.

South America. In his journal, Cook recorded his group's arrival:

> At 2 p.m. anchored in the Bay of Success in 9 fathoms . . . I went ashore accompanied by Mr. Banks and Dr. Solander to look for a watering place and to speak with the natives, who were assembled on the beach at the head of the bay to the number of 30 or 40. They were so far from being afraid or surprised at our coming amongst them that three of them came on board without the least hesitation. They are something above the middle size, of a dark copper color with long black hair; they paint their bodies in streaks, mostly red and black. Their clothing consists wholly in a guanacoe skin or that of a seal, in the same form as it came from the animal's back.[9]

On January 21, 1769, the *Endeavour* sailed out of the Bay of Good Success. Their route now took them toward Cape Horn at the very tip of South America. The area was known for its fierce winds and rough seas. Cook was surprised at the calm seas and good weather as the *Endeavour* sailed around Cape Horn. Then setting course for Tahiti, Cook and his crew sailed northwest across the Pacific Ocean.

Observing the Transit of Venus

On April 13, 1769, the *Endeavour* arrived in Tahiti, eight months after leaving England. As soon as the crew dropped anchor in Matavai Bay, hundreds of Tahitians in canoes surrounded the *Endeavour*. The Tahitians seemed happy to see the Europeans. John Gore, one of Cook's officers, had sailed to Tahiti with Captain Samuel Wallis two years earlier. Some of the Tahitians recognized Gore, thus assuring a warm welcome for those aboard the *Endeavour*.

Cook decided that a sandy spit at the northeast end of Matavai Bay would be the best place to set up his Venus transit observatory. The crew, with the willing help of the Tahitians, built walls and a gateway. Tents were pitched inside. Cook called

Cook built a transit observatory and fort at the northeast end of Matavai Bay in Tahiti in the spring of 1769. Cook observed the transit of Venus on June 3, 1769. This is a painting of Point Venus, Tahiti, 1773.

the fortified observatory Fort Venus. The location has become known as Point Venus.

At first, the Europeans and the Tahitians got along extremely well. After long months at sea, the men of the *Endeavour* were happy to have arrived at such a beautiful island. Indeed, Tahiti struck them as a tropical paradise. The Tahitians were an amazingly hospitable people. Cook and his officers dined almost nightly with the local Tahitian chiefs.

But growing tensions soon overshadowed the mutual good feelings. The Europeans realized that the Tahitians were stealing things from them. Apparently the Tahitians had no concept of private property and saw nothing wrong with stealing. They figured that if they saw something they liked, why shouldn't they just take it? Cook tried to make it clear to the Tahitians that such behavior was unacceptable.

Cook became furious when he discovered that the quadrant had been stolen. The quadrant was an astronomical instrument that was essential for observing the transit of Venus. Luckily, a local chief named Tubourai understood that the Tahitians would pay a heavy price if the quadrant was not returned. Tubourai knew the identity of the thieves, and the quadrant was quickly retrieved. Gifts were exchanged between Europeans and Tahitians, and good feelings eventually resumed.

On June 3, 1769, Cook, the astronomer Charles Green, and Daniel Solander observed the transit of Venus. According to Cook:

> This day prov'd as favourable to our purpose as we could wish, not a Clowd was to be seen the whole day and the Air was perfectly clear, so that we had every advantage we could desire in Observing the whole of the passage of the planet Venus over the Suns disk: we very distinctly saw an Atmosphere or dusky shade round the body of the Planet which very much disturbed the times of the Contacts particularly the two internal ones. Dr. Solander observed as well as Mr. Green and myself, and we differ'd from one another in observeing the times of the Contacts much more than could be expected. Mr. Greens Telescope and mine were of the same Magnifying power but that of the Dr. was greater then ours.[10]

MAPPING NEW ZEALAND

After completing the observation of the transit of Venus, Cook opened the sealed orders from the Admiralty. His instructions were to search for *Terra Australis* in the South Pacific, the mysterious unknown continent. Upon finding the continent, Cook was to claim it for Britain.

Before leaving Tahiti, Cook wanted to make a survey of the island. He and Banks, accompanied by a young local chief named Tupia, set out in a small sailboat on June 26, 1769. Cook worked

with his usual thoroughness and produced a very accurate map of the complete coastline of Tahiti. On the west coast of the island, they came across a large *marae,* a Tahitian place of worship built of stone. Cook was very impressed with the stonework. In his journal entry of July 13, 1769, he wrote: "When one considers the tools these people have to work with, one cannot help but admire their workmanship."[11] The three men returned to Fort Venus on July 1. The next month was spent making repairs on the *Endeavour* and stocking provisions.

As the *Endeavour* prepared for its departure from Tahiti, a tricky situation unfolded. Apparently, two crew members, Clement Webb and Samuel Gibson, deserted the ship and fled to the hills with their Tahitian girlfriends. Cook could not allow them to get away with this. He was aware that others among the crew might follow in their footsteps. Cook held six local chiefs hostage, pending the return of Webb and Gibson. With the help of Tahitian guides, the two seamen were located and brought back to the ship.

On August 9, 1769, the *Endeavour* sailed away from Tahiti. On board was Tupia, who would serve as a guide and translator. Cook stopped at several other neighboring islands, including Huahine, Raiatea, Bora-Bora, and Rurutu. Cook named the chain of islands the Society Islands and claimed them all for Britain. Then the *Endeavour* sailed due south. The Admiralty's instructions were to proceed as far as latitude 40° south. Upon reaching that latitude on September 2, Cook did not sight land and turned west.

On October 7, 1769, the *Endeavour* reached the east coast of New Zealand's North Island. The first to sight land was a young crew member named Nicholas Young. Cook was not the first European to see New Zealand. In 1642, the Dutch navigator and explorer Abel Tasman had sailed along part of the west coast of New Zealand. Tasman had sailed out of Batavia (present-day Jakarta, Indonesia) in the Dutch East Indies. He reached New Zealand, after having discovered Tasmania, off the southeast coast of Australia. Tasman lacked Cook's thoroughness. He had failed to sail far enough to determine if New Zealand was an island or whether it was connected to a large continent, nor did he learn if Tasmania was an island.

MEETING THE MAORI

Tasman had found the native Maori people to be so hostile that he had never attempted to go ashore. Cook, however, made several landings along the North Island coast. In so doing, he and his crew became the first Europeans to set foot in New Zealand. Cook's first encounter with the Maori ended badly. Cook had asked the Maori to

Captain Cook's chart of New Zealand from 1769–1770, the first map ever rendered of New Zealand. Cook first reached the coast of the island on October 7, 1769.

board his ship so he could speak with them. After they refused to do so, Cook's men fired several warning shots, and one of the Maori was killed.

As Cook sailed north along the New Zealand coast, he stopped at various bays along the route. Sometimes the local Maori were friendly, and Cook's men would trade with them. At other times, the Maori were hostile. In his journal entry dated November 4–12, 1769, Cook wrote: "In the Morning several Canoes came to us from all Parts of the Bay; in them were about 130 or 140 People. To all appearances their first design was to attack us, being all completely Arm'd. However after Parading about the Ship near three hours, some times trading with us and at other times tricking of us, they disperse'd but not before we had fired a few Musquets."[12]

On becoming better acquainted with the Maori, Cook expressed an appreciation for the tattooed swirls on the Maori warriors. In his journal entry of March 31, 1770, Cook wrote: "The figures they mostly use are spirals drawn and connected together with great nicety and judgment. From this I conclude that it takes perhaps years to finish the operation. The manner in which it must be done must certainly cause intolerable pain."[13]

Cook named many of New Zealand's bays and other geographical features. These included Poverty Bay, Hawke's Bay, Cape Kidnappers, Cape

Turnagain, Cape Runaway, Bay of Plenty, and Mercury Bay. At Mercury Bay, Cook and Green observed a transit of the planet Mercury.

The *Endeavour* rounded the northern tip of the North Island and headed south along the west coast. On January 11, 1770, Cook sighted an eight-thousand-foot-high mountain covered with fresh snow. He named it Mount Egmont (present-day Mount Taranaki). Soon after, on January 16, Cook sailed the *Endeavour* into a fine harbor. He anchored the ship there while the crew carried

A drawing of an exchange between a Maori trader and an English sailor from the *Endeavour* during Cook's expedition. Cook and his crew had a hot-and-cold relationship with the Maori.

out routine maintenance work. Cook named the harbor Queen Charlotte Sound.

The *Endeavour* departed Queen Charlotte Sound on February 7. Cook then sailed through the body of water between New Zealand's North and South Islands. He named this waterway Cook Strait. The *Endeavour* sailed all the way around the South Island. On the southwest corner of the South Island, Cook discovered several magnificent deep fjords. By March 27, Cook had completed a circumnavigation of the South and North Islands and had mapped the entire coastline. He claimed New Zealand for the British Crown. It was now time to continue the search for *Terra Australis*. On April 1, the *Endeavour* sailed west in hopes of finding the unknown continent.

Charting the East Coast of Australia

In 1644, Abel Tasman had made a second voyage of exploration in the South Pacific. His trips were sponsored by the Dutch East India Company, a trading company with headquarters at Batavia. Tasman's sponsors were eager to learn whether the rumored *Terra Australis* had any commercial potential. Although Tasman surveyed the northern coastline of New Holland (present-day Australia), his sponsors were disappointed with the results of the voyage. Tasman had failed to establish whether the land he charted was part of a large island or part of the great unknown southern continent. His reports of a barren landscape and primitive people discouraged all prospects of trade and settlement. As a result, Europeans showed little interest in the region throughout the next century.

On April 19, 1770, the *Endeavour* reached the southeast coast of Australia. Lieutenant Hicks was the first person to sight land. So Cook named the spot Point Hicks. The *Endeavour* then sailed north along the coast. On April 29, the crew found a suitable harbor for anchoring the ship and ventured ashore. Cook named the harbor Stingray Bay because the water was filled with stingrays.

As the men prepared to row ashore, they noticed a settlement near the beach. There were several huts near some trees. The inhabitants went about their business, seeming to take no notice of the *Endeavour*. Cook and several others got into a longboat and began rowing toward shore. They saw that a group of Aborigine men had gathered on the beach and were watching as the Englishmen approached the shore. They did not look very friendly.

The artist Sydney Parkinson described this first meeting between the Englishmen and the Aborigines. He wrote:

Their countenance bespoke displeasure; they threatened us, and discovered hostile intentions, often crying to us Warra warra wai. We made signs to them to be peaceable, and threw them some trinkets; but they kept aloof and dared us to come ashore. We attempted to frighten them by firing off a gun loaded with small shot, but attempted it in vain. One of them repaired to a house immediately and brought out a shield, of an oval figure, painted white in the middle, with two holes in the middle to see through, and also a wooden sword, and then they advanced boldly, gathering up stones as they came along, which they threw at us.[14]

When they reached the beach, Cook gave Isaac Smith, his wife's young nephew, the honor of being the first to step ashore. By the time all were on shore, the Aborigines had fled. Cook regretted being unable to make contact with them during his stay. Meanwhile, Banks, Solander, and the other scientists were pleased with the local flora. They collected hundreds of specimens of plants that were unknown in Europe. Cook was so impressed with the profusion of plants that he changed the name of Stingray Bay to Botany Bay.

On May 6, 1770, the *Endeavour* left Botany Bay and sailed north along the coast. On June 11, the *Endeavour* ran aground in the Great Barrier Reef. Luckily, Cook and his crew managed to get the ship free of the reef. On June 17, the *Endeavour* reached the shore, where all the necessary repairs were made. For the first time, Cook established a degree of understanding with the Aborigines. The scientists of the *Endeavour* made the first major collection of Australian plants. They saw several species of animals for the first time, too. These animals included crocodiles, flying foxes, dingoes, wallabies, and kangaroos. They got the word *kangaroo* from the local Aborigines.

On August 13, 1770, the *Endeavour* set sail again. Cook continued to head north along the

A sailor carves HMS *Endeavour* in a tree as Captain Cook commemorates the landing of the *Endeavour* in Botany Bay in April 1770.

coast of Australia. As they traveled, he made charts of the entire east coast of Australia and adjacent waters. On August 22, the *Endeavour* rounded the northernmost point of the Cape York Peninsula. Cook landed on a nearby island. There, he officially took possession of the vast coastal region he had just mapped for the British Crown. He gave the appropriate name Possession Island to the small island. Later, he gave the name New South Wales to the eastern part of Australia.

Cook then sailed through Torres Strait between Australia and New Guinea, proving that the two landmasses were not part of a single continent. On October 11, 1770, the *Endeavour* anchored at Batavia in present-day Indonesia. The ship needed repairs and fresh supplies. Unfortunately, there was an outbreak of malaria at Batavia. Many of the men aboard the *Endeavour*, who had so far avoided falling victim to scurvy, now succumbed to malaria and dysentery.

On December 26, the *Endeavour* left Batavia and sailed west toward Africa. After sailing around the Cape of Good Hope at the southern tip of Africa, the *Endeavour* arrived at Cape Town on March 14, 1771. About thirty of Cook's crew had to be put ashore in a hospital. Cook found seamen in Cape Town to replace his sick crewmen. On April 16, the *Endeavour* departed Cape Town, bound for England.

On July 13, 1771, the *Endeavour* reached England. After three years, the long journey was over. Cook had charted two thousand miles of the New Zealand coastline. He had proved that New Zealand consisted of two separate islands and, therefore, could not be part of a continental land-mass. He had also been the first person to navigate the Great Barrier Reef and chart the east coast of Australia.

Captain Cook saw many animals unknown to Europeans in Australia, including the kangaroo. This is an engraving from Captain Cook's *Account of a Voyage Round the World in the Years 1768–1771.*

The Royal Society was thrilled with all the specimens and drawings that Banks and Solander had brought back. There were hundreds of plants previously unknown in England. There were also skins of animals and birds, fish, and countless numbers of insects, all unfamiliar in Europe.

Although Banks and Solander basked in instant fame, Cook was relatively modest about what he had achieved. Upon his return, he wrote to the Admiralty: "I flatter myself that the discoveries we have made, tho' not great, will apologize for the length of the voyage."[15] To his friend and former employer John Walker of Whitby, Cook wrote: "I however have made no very great Discoveries, yet I have explor'd more of the Great South Sea than all that have gone before me so much that little remains now to be done to have a thorough knowledge of that part of the Globe."[16]

Soon, Cook realized that quite a bit more than "little" remained to be done. Before long, he would embark on his next voyage of exploration.

Chapter 4

The Search for the Unknown Continent

Upon returning to England after his first Pacific voyage, James Cook was happy to be reunited with his family. But he was not destined to remain in England long. His first voyage had done much to dispel belief in the myth of the Great Southern Continent. But some members of the Royal Society were unconvinced.

Cook's charts of the east coast of Australia showed a landmass that was continental in size. But the mythical *Terra Australis* was supposed to lie farther south than Australia. If the unknown continent could not be found in the western Pacific, perhaps it was located in the eastern Pacific. So the Royal Society Admiralty chose Cook to lead another expedition. He was to sail around the globe at the farthest southern latitudes possible. He would explore the far southern reaches of the Atlantic, Pacific, and Indian oceans. In so doing, he would discover once and for all whether a great southern continent existed south of Australia.

Another Pacific Voyage

Cook's near disaster in the Great Barrier Reef showed the risks of exploring with only one ship. So the new expedition was provided with two ships. Cook commanded HMS *Resolution*. Like the *Endeavour*, the *Resolution* was a Whitby collier, a wide ship with a flat bottom and shallow draft. Like the *Endeavour*, it was especially suitable for sailing close to shore, thereby facilitating the charting of coasts.

Accompanying the *Resolution* on the voyage was HMS *Adventure,* also a Whitby collier. It was commanded by Tobias Furneaux, who would be following Cook's orders. Furneaux was an experienced explorer who had previously sailed around the world with Samuel Wallis.

On July 13, 1772, the *Resolution* and the *Adventure* departed from Plymouth, England. The crews had been carefully selected. Sailing with Cook on the *Resolution* were eleven officers who had served under his command on the *Endeavour*. Joseph Banks wanted to go and had the ship renovated to suit his needs. But the changes he made were declared unseaworthy, and the ship was changed back. Banks refused to go. So Cook hired the German botanist Johann Reinhold Förster, who took along his seventeen-year-old son Georg as his assistant. Also on board were the astronomer William Wales and the artist William Hodges. Sailing with Cook for the second time was Elizabeth Cook's nephew Isaac Smith.

On the eve of his departure, Cook wrote to his friend John Walker at Whitby:

> Having nothing new to communicate I should hardly have troubled you with a letter was it not customary for Men to take leave of their friends before they go out of the World, for I can hardly think myself in it so long as I am deprived from having any Connections with the civilized part of it and this will soon be my case for two years at least. When I think of the Inhospitable parts I am going to, I think the Voyage dangerous, I however enter upon it with great cheerfulness, providence has been very kind to me on many occasions, and I trust in the continuation of the divine protection; I have two good Ships well provided and well Man'd.[1]

On his second voyage, Cook would have a new method of determining his precise geographical position. He would become the first commander of a ship in history to know almost exactly where he was on the earth's surface, even after many months without seeing land. Up until now, Cook could always determine his latitude, or degrees north or south of the equator. As long as he knew what day of the year it was, he could consult his charts of the sun's position for each day. Then, by using his sextant to measure the angle between the sun and the horizon, he could calculate the latitude. However, now Cook carried with him an extremely reliable clock called a chronometer.

It would always give the correct time at the Greenwich meridian. He could then compare Greenwich time with his local time to determine longitude, or degrees east or west of Greenwich, England.

In 1761, John Harrison, a Yorkshire clockmaker, had invented a clock called a chronometer that would be unaffected by storms at sea or by large changes of temperature and humidity. On his second voyage, Cook carried a replica of Harrison's clock, made by Larcum Kendall in 1769. In his journal, Cook described his timepiece as "our

Chronometers used on Captain Cook's second voyage. This tool helped Cook determine his precise geographical location.

trusty guide the watch . . . it would not be doing justice to Mr. Harrison and Mr. Kendall, if I did not own that we have received very great assistance from this useful and valuable time-piece."[2]

On his first voyage, Cook had reached the Pacific by sailing west. This time, he would take an easterly route to reach the Pacific. Cook's plan was to sail in extreme southern latitudes during the summer months, which corresponded to winter months in the Northern Hemisphere. This way the expedition would avoid the severe cold of the Antarctic winter. The rest of the time, Cook planned to search for undiscovered islands, using Tahiti and New Zealand as ports. He would also try to find islands that had been discovered in earlier expeditions but whose locations had never been properly marked. Due to more primitive navigation techniques in the past, the charts of those early explorers were often inaccurate. Some charts were lost.

BOUND FOR THE ANTARCTIC

On October 30, 1772, the *Resolution* and the *Adventure* sailed into Table Bay at Cape Town, near the southern tip of Africa. Cook and Furneaux restocked the provisions on the two ships. On November 22, they left Cape Town, bound for the Antarctic.

As the *Resolution* and the *Adventure* sailed farther south, the weather grew steadily worse.

Gale force winds alternated with periods of dense icy fog. The ships sailed through high seas, while cold rains turned to hail, sleet, and then snow. Icicles formed on the rigging and sails as the temperature kept dropping. By early December, the seas around the ships became filled with icebergs. The huge chunks of floating ice struck fear in the men aboard.

In his journal of December 12, 1772, Cook wrote:

> We were obliged to proceed with great caution on account of the ice islands. Six of these we passed this day; some of them near two miles in circuit, and sixty feet high. And yet, such was the force and height of the waves, that the sea broke quite over them. This exhibited a view which for a few moments was pleasing to the eye; but then we reflected on the danger, the mind was filled with horror. For were a ship to get against the weather-side of one of these islands when the sea runs high, she would be dashed to pieces in a moment.[3]

On January 17, 1773, the two ships, still heading south, crossed the Antarctic Circle. This was the first time anybody had sailed that far south. But the following day, the thickening sea ice stopped them from sailing any farther south. At noon, they were 4.5 miles inside the Antarctic Circle. Although Cook did not know it, they were only about 150 miles from what is now known as Crown Prince Olaf Land in Antarctica.

From the masthead, Cook reported an almost unbroken field of ice to the south and also to the east and west. He realized that if they attempted to go any farther south, or even stay where they were, the ships could be trapped in the ice for many months. So Cook ordered a retreat to the north.

On February 8, a thick fog closed in on the ships. When the weather finally cleared the next day, the *Adventure* was nowhere to be seen. Cook expected they would rendezvous later with the *Adventure* at Queen Charlotte Sound in New Zealand. They had previously agreed to this plan in case the two ships were separated. So the *Resolution* sailed across the southern Indian Ocean toward New Zealand.

On his second voyage, Captain Cook sailed the *Resolution* and *Adventure* south across the Antarctic Circle. This was the farthest south anyone had ever sailed.

On March 23, 1773, the *Resolution* arrived in Dusky Bay (present-day Dusky Sound), New Zealand. Cook stayed at Dusky Bay long enough for his crew to recuperate from the hardships they had endured at sea. After not seeing land for four months, they were happy to go ashore. The Maori were friendly, fish and wildfowl were abundant, and there was plenty of fresh drinking water. On May 19, 1773, the *Resolution* reunited with the *Adventure* at Queen Charlotte Sound.

No Sign of the Southern Continent

Cook planned to sail east to the middle of the Pacific. If the mythical continent did not materialize, they would head to Tahiti to take on fresh supplies. Both ships left New Zealand on June 7, 1773, heading east. They sailed about three thousand miles across a large area of the Pacific. Finding no trace of a continent, Cook then headed north toward Tahiti.

On August 17, 1773, the *Resolution* and *Adventure* arrived in Tahiti. Those who had sailed with Cook on his last voyage were happy to see familiar faces among the Tahitians. The Englishmen spent about a month on Tahiti and some of the other Society Islands. Then on September 18, 1773, Cook and Furneaux sailed away, heading west.

Cook sighted a group of islands that later became known as the Cook Islands. He then reached the islands of present-day Tonga. The people of the Tongan Islands gave an especially warm welcome to the Englishmen. Because of this, Cook named these islands the Friendly Islands. After spending some time ashore, the two crews prepared to sail. Upon departing the Friendly Islands, Cook headed back toward New Zealand.

On October 24, 1773, the *Resolution* and the *Adventure* were approaching Cook Strait when they were caught in a fierce gale. The stormy weather lasted for a week. On October 30, there was no sign of the *Adventure*. Cook sailed the *Resolution* into Queen Charlotte Sound. Once the *Resolution* anchored, the crew began repairing the battered ship. During the next few weeks, the crew stored fresh supplies of food and water on the ship. By November 25, there was still no sign of the *Adventure*. So Cook decided to leave New Zealand and head for the Antarctic again.

Before leaving Queen Charlotte Sound, Cook left a message for Furneaux, in case the *Adventure* should arrive there later. In his message, Cook described his planned course. He left the message in a bottle that he buried in the ground beneath a tree near their anchoring cove. On the tree, Cook carved the words LOOK UNDERNEATH.

As it happened, Cook and Furneaux missed each other by a few days. When the *Adventure*

Engraved for MILLAR's SYSTEM of

New Complete & Universal GEOGRAPHY.

A Chief and other Natives of O'Taheitee, visiting Capt. Cook in his second Voyage to the Southern Hemisphere.

Tahitians visiting Captain Cook on the deck of the *Resolution* in August 1773. Cook's crew was happy to see some familiar faces in Tahiti.

reached Queen Charlotte Sound, the *Resolution* had already sailed. Furneaux did find Cook's message in the bottle. Cook had written that he might try to reach Easter Island and then probably the Society Islands again. But there were no specific instructions as to a rendezvous. So Furneaux decided to head home. But before sailing, his crew had a violent encounter with the local Maori. Eleven of Furneaux's men were killed. Furneaux eventually made it back to England, arriving home a year ahead of Cook.

● BACK TO THE ANTARCTIC

Meanwhile, Cook headed south toward the Antarctic. The farther south the *Resolution* sailed, the colder it got. By December, hail, sleet, freezing fog, and snow made life difficult for the crew. A crewman named Jack Marra wrote: "Icicles frequently hung to the noses of the men more than an inch long, the men cased in frozen snow, as if clad in armour, where the running rigging has been so enlarged by frozen sleet as hardly to be grasped by the largest hand . . ."[4]

The first iceberg appeared on December 12, 1773. During the next few weeks, more icebergs clogged the sea. On January 26, 1774, the *Resolution* crossed the Antarctic Circle for the second time and continued heading south. But on January 30, 1774, Cook decided it was time to turn back.

A field of ice blocked their path that stretched ahead as far as the eye could see. On the southern horizon, what appeared to be mountains of ice rose up into the clouds. The *Resolution*'s position was 71° 10′ south latitude and 106° 54′ west longitude. They were about 350 miles south of the Antarctic Circle. They were less than one hundred miles from the Thurston Peninsula on the Antarctic continent.

In his journal, Cook wrote:

> It was indeed my opinion as well as the opinion of most on board, that this ice extended quite to the Pole or perhaps joined on some land, to which it had been fixed from the earliest time. . . . I who had ambition not only to go farther than anyone had been before, but as far as it was possible for man to go, was not sorry at meeting with this interruption, as it in some measure relieved us, at least shortened the dangers and hardships inseparable from the navigation of the southern polar regions. . . . [5]

ISLAND HOPPING IN THE PACIFIC

Because it was too late in the season to sail around Cape Horn to explore the South Atlantic, Cook decided to visit more islands in the Pacific, including some that had been discovered by earlier explorers. One of these was Easter Island, also known as Rapa Nui. The *Resolution* arrived there on March 11, 1774. Cook and his men marveled at the mysterious giant stone statues that had been erected at various points along the shore.

Cook was also amazed that the natives of Rapa Nui spoke a language clearly related to that of the Maori and the Tahitians, even though the islands were thousands of miles apart. Cook wrote: "It is extraordinary that the same Nation should have spread themselves over all the isles in this Vast Ocean from New Zealand to this Island which is almost a fourth part of the circumference of the Globe."[6]

Captain Cook reached Easter Island on March 11, 1774. Cook and his crew marveled at the ancient stone statues they saw on the island. The statues still stand there today.

From Easter Island, Cook went on to Norfolk Island and the Marquesas Islands. He then stopped again in Tahiti to resupply his ship. Next he visited the New Hebrides, present-day Vanuatu. Until then, the peoples of all the islands Cook had visited were Polynesian. The natives of the New Hebrides, however, were known as Melanesians. They were physically different from Polynesians and spoke an unrelated language. On his way back to New Zealand, Cook discovered the large island of New Caledonia.

On October 18, 1774, the *Resolution* was back at Ship Cove in Queen Charlotte Sound, New Zealand. Cook retrieved the bottle he had left with a message for Furneaux. Now the bottle was empty. So Cook was pleased to learn that the *Adventure* had made it to Ship Cove and, hopefully, back to England. But then Cook learned from the local Maori about the casualties among Furneaux's crew. Cook was horrified to learn that the eleven unlucky seamen had been eaten by the Maori warriors after they had been murdered. Cook had previously seen evidence of cannibalism among the Maori and people of some of the other islands. Apparently it was the custom on certain occasions to eat the flesh of enemies one has killed. Nevertheless, Cook guessed that Furneaux's men must have insulted the Maori in such a way as to bring on the attack. Cook wrote: "I shall

make no reflection on this melancholy affair until I hear more about it. I must, however, observe in favour of the New Zealanders that I have always found them of a brave, noble, open and benevolent disposition, but they are a people who will never put up with an insult if they have an opportunity to resent it."[7]

On November 10, 1774, Cook left New Zealand and sailed east. By December 25, the *Resolution* had rounded Cape Horn and arrived in Tierra del Fuego. On January 3, 1775, Cook made a third and final sweep of the Antarctic and then sailed east across the South Atlantic to Cape Town.

Cook was convinced that if a continent did exist far to the south, it would be impossible to get there because of the ice. And, of course, such a place would be totally inhospitable and therefore useless to humans. Cook wrote:

> [T]he greatest part of this southern continent (supposing there is one) must lie within the polar circle, where the sea is so pestered with ice that the land is thereby inaccessible. The risk one runs in exploring a coast in these unknown and icy seas, is so very great, that I can be bold to say that no man will ever venture farther than I have done; and that the lands which may lie to the south will never be explored.[8]

On April 27, 1775, Cook left Cape Town and headed north toward home. On July 29, 1775, the *Resolution* reached England.

Cook had covered about sixty thousand miles on his three-year voyage. This was equal to two and a half times the circumference of the earth. Cook had accomplished a great deal. He had proved that a large, habitable continent did not exist in the earth's extreme southern latitudes. His charts of the southern Pacific Ocean were so accurate that copies of them were still in use in the mid-twentieth century.

In describing the major accomplishment of his second voyage, Cook wrote:

> I had now made the circuit of the Southern Ocean in a high Latitude and traversed it in such manner as to leave not the least room for the Possibility of there being a continent, unless near the Pole and out of the reach of Navigation; by twice visiting the Pacific Tropical Sea, I had not only settled the situation of some old discoveries but made there many new ones, and left, I conceive, very little more to be done even in that part.[9]

Cook's journeys had brought him fame. On August 9, 1775, Cook was promoted to captain. His commission was personally handed to him by King George III. On February 29, 1776, Cook was elected a Fellow of the Royal Society. The Society then awarded Cook the Copley Medal for his contribution to the health of seamen. Although one of Cook's men had died from illness on the long voyage, nobody on the *Resolution* had died from scurvy.

In his journal, Cook wrote:

[O]ur having discovered the possibility of preserving health amongst a numerous ship's company for such a length of time in such varieties of climate and amidst such continued hardship and fatigue will make this voyage remarkable in the opinion of every benevolent person when the dispute about a southern continent shall have ceased to engage the attention and divide the judgement of philosophers.[10]

Chapter 5

The Fateful Pacific Expedition

Captain
James Cook was home again, happy to be reunited with his wife and three sons. As a reward for completing his three-year voyage of discovery, Cook was appointed to run Greenwich Hospital, a largely ceremonial position. The position was his for the rest of his life, should he so desire. It offered financial security.

As Cook went to work at his new job, he wondered if it suited him. In a letter Cook sent to his friend John Walker, he wrote:

> [M]y fate drives me from one extream to another a few Months ago the whole Southern hemisphere was hardly big enough for me and now I am going to be confined within the limits of Greenwich hospital, which are far too small for an active mind like mine, I must however confess it is a fine retreat and a pretty income, but whether I can bring my self to like ease and retirement, time will shew.[1]

Indeed, it did not take long until Cook made up his mind. He attended a dinner on January 9, 1776, hosted by the Earl of Sandwich, the First Lord of the Admiralty. The discussion over dinner concerned plans for a new voyage of discovery. The naval officials talked about who they should appoint to command the expedition. They discussed Charles Clerke, who had sailed with Cook on the *Endeavour* and then on the *Resolution*. Other names came up. But at the end of the evening, Cook stood up and announced, "I will myself undertake the direction of this enterprise if I am so commanded."[2] Of course, the officials were delighted to oblige Cook.

BACK TO THE PACIFIC

Cook's third voyage had a different goal than the previous two. The Admiralty wanted to find out if a Northwest Passage existed between the Pacific and Atlantic oceans. Such a waterway across the top of North America, if it existed, would enable British ships to reach Asia by a much shorter and more direct route. They would no longer have to sail all the way around Cape Horn or the Cape of Good Hope. The British economy would benefit from expanded trade.

Cook's voyage would also give Britain knowledge of new lands in North America with the potential for British settlement. The conflict for control of Britain's colonies on the east coast of North America had already begun, as many colonists were determined to fight for their independence from Britain. Meanwhile on the west coast, Russian hunters and traders were already active in Alaska. So it was clearly in Britain's interest to learn as much as possible about this part of the world.

On June 25, 1776, Cook's third voyage to the Pacific began. Like the second voyage, this expedition consisted of two ships. Cook again commanded the *Resolution*. Sailing with Cook was William Bligh, who would one day become famous when his crew on HMS *Bounty* mutinied. Also on board were the physician and naturalist William Anderson, the artist John Webber, and two American seamen, John Gore and John Ledyard. Gore had previously sailed with Cook. The other important person on the ship was George Vancouver, who would later command his own ships into the Pacific and map Hawaii and British Columbia in much greater detail.

Charles Clerke was put in charge of the second ship, the *Discovery*. But the *Discovery*'s departure was delayed until a later date. Meanwhile Cook sailed south to Cape Town. Repairs were made there on the *Resolution* while Cook waited for the *Discovery*. The *Discovery* eventually arrived at Cape Town, and the two ships departed on December 1, 1776.

Cook's route during the next year took him from island to island, as he cruised the Pacific. Some places he revisited, other islands were new discoveries. In January 1777, Cook spent four days at Adventure Bay, Tasmania. Next, he spent about two weeks in February at Queen Charlotte Sound, New Zealand. There, the local Maori were nervous when Cook arrived. They expected he had come to seek revenge for the killing of Furneaux's crewmen. But Cook treated the Maori with respect, and there were no further problems.

Cook then hoped to sail the nearly nine thousand miles to the Bering Strait in the far north. But upon leaving New Zealand, the winds were blowing in the wrong direction. There would not be enough time to reach the north before the Arctic winter began. So Cook decided to visit more Pacific islands instead and sail north the following year.

In July, Cook revisited the Friendly Islands. In August, Cook returned to Tahiti, where he remained until December. On December 25, 1777, Cook discovered another new island, which he appropriately named Christmas Island.

On January 18, 1778, as Cook sailed north, he made one of his most important discoveries. The *Resolution* and the *Discovery* had come upon another previously uncharted group of islands. Oahu, Kauai, and then the small island Niihau were sighted first. Cook headed for Kauai, where they dropped anchor near a settlement called Waimea. The Hawaiians had never seen a ship

On January 18, 1778, Cook became the first European to land on the Hawaiian Islands. He dropped anchor near a settlement called Waimea. This is the present-day Waimea Bay.

from Europe before. Apparently, they also may have thought that Cook was a god-king figure.

Cook realized that the people of these islands had a similar language and culture as the Tahitians. He named the island group the Sandwich Islands, after the Earl of Sandwich. Today, they are called the Hawaiian Islands.

Exploring the West Coast of North America

After fresh food and water were loaded on the *Resolution* and the *Discovery,* the ships sailed away, heading northeast. On March 6, 1778, Cook and his crew sighted land. The two ships had reached New Albion (North America), at a point along the coast of present-day Oregon. The weather was so bad that Cook named the spot Cape Foul Weather. Cook observed hills and valleys, almost everywhere covered with woods. Noting that there was nothing remarkable, Cook sailed north along the coast. Their progress was slowed by heavy rain and gale winds.

On March 29, the two ships anchored at Nootka Sound in what is now British Columbia. Some Nootka Indians in canoes approached the ships, chanting as they paddled. The Indians welcomed the visitors by singing what seemed to be a song of greeting. They were eager for trade with those on the ships. According to Cook, "We had

CAPTAIN COOK AT NOOTKA, 1778

Cook and his crew meeting with Nootka Indians on Vancouver Island, Canada, in March 1778.

the company of the natives all day, who now laid aside all manner of restraint, if they ever had any, and came on board the Ships and mixed with our people with the greatest freedom."[3] From then on, relations between both peoples were friendly.

Cook stayed in their sheltered cove in Nootka Sound long enough to make urgently needed repairs on the *Resolution*. Almost a month later, on April 26, the two ships left Nootka Sound. They sailed north, in rough seas and weather that was frequently bad. On May 30, they entered what is now called Cook Inlet. They sailed up the inlet for several hundred miles until the surrounding mountains closed in on them. They were near the site of present-day Anchorage, Alaska. On June 6, a disappointed Cook wrote in his journal that he had been "induced very much against my own opinion and judgment, to pursue the Course I did, as it was the opinion of some of the Officers that we should certainly find passage to the North."[4]

The *Resolution* and the *Discovery* sailed southwest along the Alaska Peninsula and then the Aleutian Islands. On August 3, 1778, William Anderson, a physician and a keen observer of human culture aboard the *Resolution,* died of tuberculosis. Cook sailed across the Bering Strait and anchored in a sheltered inlet on the Siberian side of the Strait. Next, Cook sailed north through the

A feather god mask from Hawaii. This mask was collected during Captain Cook's third Pacific voyage. The artifact actually has human hair.

Bering Strait, crossing the Arctic Circle. The two ships now continued north into the Chukchi Sea, an arm of the Arctic Ocean. As in the Antarctic on Cook's previous voyage, the sea became filled with icebergs. The farther north they went, the colder it became.

On August 17, 1778, the expedition faced a wall of ice about twelve feet high that extended from the eastern to the western horizon. They had reached the latitude of 70° 44′ north. Cook sailed back and forth, looking for an opening in the ice. But he could find none. So he decided that they would sail back to the Hawaiian Islands. After spending the winter there, they would head north again. Hopefully, the next year they would have better luck in finding the Northwest Passage.

THE END IN THE HAWAIIAN ISLANDS

On October 2, 1778, Cook stopped at Unalaska, a Russian settlement in the Aleutian Islands. Cook found the Russians to be friendly and hospitable. On October 14, the Russian governor of the settlement came aboard the *Resolution*. He and Cook were able to exchange information using sign language, since neither one spoke the other's language.

On October 26, Captain Cook sailed south from Unalaska. The next day, Cook celebrated his fiftieth birthday. He was disappointed he had not found the Northwest Passage. But this failure gave him the opportunity to revisit the Hawaiian Islands. He believed that his discovery of these islands was the most important that had yet been made by Europeans throughout the Pacific Ocean.

The two ships reached the Hawaiian Islands on November 26. As they sailed along the coast of Maui, Hawaiians in canoes approached the ships. On November 30, a chief named Terreeoboo came aboard the *Resolution.* He gave Cook some piglets. In the evening, Cook sighted another island to the south. It was a much bigger island, with two massive snow-covered volcanoes that rise to nearly fourteen thousand feet. The Hawaiians told Cook that this island was called Owhyhee (Hawaii).

The *Resolution* and the *Discovery* sailed all around the coast of the Big Island of Hawaii. On January 16, 1779, the two ships sailed into Kealakekua Bay and dropped anchor. In his journal entry of January 17, Cook wrote:

> At 11 o'clock in the forenoon we anchored in thirteen fathoms of water in the bay which is called by the natives Karakakooa. The ships [became] much crowded with natives, and were surrounded by a multitude of canoes. I had nowhere, in the course

of my voyages, seen so numerous a body of people assembled at one place. Besides those who had come off to us in canoes, all the shore of the bay was covered with spectators, and hundreds were swimming round the ship like shoals of fish. We could not but be struck with the singularity of this scene.[5]

A priest named Koa and two chiefs came aboard and gave Cook an offering of two coconuts and a small pig. Later, when Cook went ashore, Koa led him to a sacred area. The Hawaiians enacted an elaborate religious ceremony, in which Cook willingly participated. The ceremony was dedicated to Lono, the Hawaiian god of peace, light, and abundance. It seems likely that the Hawaiians believed Cook to be the incarnation of Lono. Cook had arrived in Hawaii during *makahiki,* the festive season of worship of Lono. Lono's symbol was a wooden staff with a square banner of cloth secured to the crossbar. The Hawaiians saw a resemblance between Lono's staff and the masts, spars, and sails of the expedition's ships. Also according to legend, Lono would one day return to his people bearing gifts. Cook had distributed various gifts—trinkets and iron objects.

On February 4, 1779, the *Resolution* and the *Discovery* departed from Kealakekua Bay. They were bound again for the Arctic in search of the Northwest Passage. But on February 8, a tremendous gust of wind struck the *Resolution,* splitting

Cook participated in a religious ceremony dedicated to Lono, the Hawaiian god of peace, light, and abundance.

the foremast. Only half of the ship's sails were now usable. Cook ordered both ships to return to the sheltered harbor at Kealakekua Bay, where the *Resolution* could be repaired.

Back at Kealakekua Bay, Cook noticed that something had changed in their absence. It was strangely quiet, with few canoes out on the bay. Perhaps the Hawaiians had been told to stay away from the ships.

DEATH OF A CAPTAIN

During the next few days, relations between the Europeans and the Hawaiians were marked by increasing tensions. The Hawaiians did not seem happy to see the Europeans. The festive season of Lono had ended. Previously the Hawaiians had been generous in sharing their resources with their visitors. Perhaps the Europeans had depleted local food supplies. Now the Hawaiians might have been afraid the Europeans would require them to supply still more food.

It became clear that the Hawaiians' earlier reverence for the visitors had been replaced by increased contempt. There was a shift in power on the island so that Cook's allies could no longer hold sway over the people, and a more hostile group was in control. The Hawaiians began stealing things at every opportunity. A number of quarrels broke out between the two groups.

On February 14, 1779, some Hawaiians stole one of Cook's small boats. Cook went ashore to retrieve the boat and a pair of tongs that had been stolen the day before. He also planned to take an important local chief hostage to help get those things back. He was met by a huge angry crowd that had gathered on the beach. When the Hawaiians began throwing stones, Cook and his men fired some shots. As the Hawaiians began attacking with spears, Cook and his crew retreated to the water's edge. Cook then turned his back to help launch the boats. Suddenly a Hawaiian struck Cook on the head. As he fell to the ground, another Hawaiian stabbed him. When Cook tried to get up, he received a mighty blow to the head. As he lay there dying, he was stabbed again.

Cook's men had been unable to save him. As the Hawaiians dragged Cook's body away, the crewmen were able to row back to the *Resolution*. The crews of both ships were shocked and saddened by the death of their leader. They retaliated by bombarding the local area with cannon fire, burning homes, and killing people. They appealed to the Hawaiians for the return of Cook's remains, and the two sides eventually agreed. Cook was given a formal burial at sea in Kealakekua Bay on February 22, 1779.

On February 14, 1779, Captain Cook was killed by Hawaiians. This rendering of the event was made in 1790.

Under Clerke's command, the expedition sailed north again through the Bering Strait. As a tribute to Cook, Clerke intended to try again to find the Northwest Passage. Clerke commanded the *Resolution,* and John Gore was in charge of the *Discovery*. Once in the Arctic, the expedition found itself battling the ice. Just as before, the ships had to turn back before being trapped in the ice. Clerke died of tuberculosis before the journey ended. Gore took over command of the expedition. The *Resolution* and the *Discovery* returned to England on October 4, 1780.

Unfortunately, Cook never found the Northwest Passage. But there was no Northwest Passage to find. Such an ice-free waterway did not and does not exist. However, some scientists believe that due to global warming, the Arctic Ocean may be entirely free of ice during the summer months in the future.

Chapter 6

A Captain's Legacy

Captain James Cook is universally recognized as being one of the world's greatest explorers. In recognition of his accomplishments, schools, universities, and hospitals in a number of countries have been named after the captain. In England, the Royal Research Ship RRS *James Cook* was built in 2006 to replace the RRS *Charles Darwin* in the United Kingdom's Royal Research Fleet.

Memorial statues and monuments to Cook appear in many places. There is a memorial statue of Cook at the Catani Gardens St. Kilda in Victoria, Australia. There is a statue of Cook in Greenwich, London, England. There is a Captain Cook monument in Corner Brook, Newfoundland. There is also one in the inner harbor in Victoria, British Columbia. A statue of James Cook stands in Waimea, Kauai, in memory of his first contact with the Hawaiian Islands. And on the Big Island in Hawaii, there is a white obelisk in honor of Cook at the site where he was killed.

Captain James Cook and the various scientists and artists on his voyages

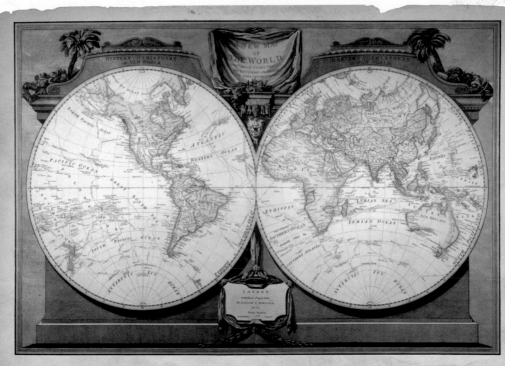

This double hemisphere map was made in 1808, recording all of
Captain Cook's voyages.

added immeasurably to the world's knowledge of the peoples, the lands, and the flora and fauna of the Pacific region. Cook's pioneering use of the new chronometers paved the way for vastly improved navigation on the seas, making it much easier to reach a particular destination. His accurate charts of thousands of miles of coastlines provided vital information for shipping.

IMPACT ON THE PEOPLES OF THE PACIFIC

Wherever he went on his voyages, Cook made serious efforts to understand the cultures of the native peoples. He was the first European to have extensive contact with many of the peoples of the Pacific islands. He correctly concluded that there was a relationship among the Polynesians, despite their being separated by thousands of miles.

Cook's discoveries would eventually lead to European settlement of various parts of the Pacific. Botanist Joseph Banks, who sailed with Cook on his first voyage, became a strong promoter of the settlement of Australia by the British. The British would also settle in New Zealand, the French in Tahiti, and the Americans in Hawaii.

With settlement came the various effects of civilization: disease and destruction of native cultural tradition by zealous Christian missionaries. Within eighty years of Cook's voyages, the population of

Tahiti decreased from forty thousand to nine thousand. By the year 1900, Australia's coastal Aborigines had been virtually wiped out.

The native peoples who survived, in such places as Australia, New Zealand, and Hawaii, became second-class citizens in their own lands. According to writer Tony Horwitz, "Many of the lands Cook claimed for Britain became wretched colonial outposts. Dispossession, like disease, must be counted as one of Cook's legacies."[1] In recent years, however, there has been a renewed interest among many native peoples of the Pacific in preserving their cultural heritage.

Cook himself realized some of the negative effects his voyages had brought to the Pacific islanders. According to Horwitz, "At times on the third voyage, he showed signs of disillusion with the whole business of exploration, and with the ills his own discoveries had brought to native peoples: disease, greed, thievery, prostitution."[2] According to historian Bernard Smith, "Cook increasingly realized that wherever he went he was spreading the curses much more liberally than the benefits of European civilization."[3]

About the Maori of New Zealand, Cook wrote: "We debauch their morals already too prone to vice and we introduce among them wants and perhaps diseases which they never before knew and which

Aboriginal women perform the Woggan-ma-gule morning ceremony on Australia day in Sydney, Australia, on January 26, 2007. The impact of Cook's voyages on the Aborigines of Australia would be disastrous.

serves only to disturb that happy tranquility they and their forefathers have enjoyed."[4]

Cook undoubtedly regretted the negative impact of his voyages because of his respect for the native peoples and his Christian beliefs. About the Aborigines of Australia, Cook wrote:

> They may appear to some to be the most wretched people upon Earth, but in reality they are far more happier than we Europeans: being wholly unacquainted not only with the superfluous but the necessary Conveniences so much sought after in Europe, they are happy in not knowing the use of them. They live in a Tranquility which is not disturb'd by the Inequality of Condition: The Earth and sea of their own accord furnishes them with all things necessary for life. . . . They seem'd to set no Value upon any thing we gave them, nor would they ever part with any thing of their own for any one article we could offer them; this in my opinion argues that they think themselves provided with all the necessarys of Life.[5]

Chapter Notes

Chapter 1. A Desperate Situation

1. Richard Hough, *Captain James Cook* (New York: W. W. Norton & Company, 1994), p. 147.

2. Ibid.

3. Ibid.

4. Tony Horwitz, *Blue Latitudes* (New York: Henry Holt, 2002), p. 167.

5. Nicholas Thomas, *Cook: The Extraordinary Voyages of Captain James Cook* (New York: Walker & Company, 2003), pp. 116–117.

6. Ibid., p. 117.

7. James Cook, "Captain Cook's Journal During His First Voyage Round the World Made in H.M. Bark 'Endeavour' 1769–71," n.d., <http://www.gutenberg.org/files/8106/8106-h/8106-h.htm> (February 2, 2009).

Chapter 2. The Call of the Sea

1. William R. Gray, *Voyages to Paradise: Exploring in the Wake of Captain Cook* (Washington, D.C.: The National Geographic Society, 1981), p. 12.

2. J. C. Beaglehole, *The Life of Captain James Cook* (Stanford, Calif.: Stanford University Press, 1974), p. 15.

3. Richard Hough, *Captain James Cook* (New York: W. W. Norton & Company, 1994), p. 13.

4. Ibid., p. 22.

Chapter 3. A Pacific Voyage

1. Richard Hough, *Captain James Cook* (New York: W. W. Norton & Company, 1994), pp. 25–26.

2. Ibid., p. 31.

3. Ibid., p. 33.

4. James Cook, "Captain Cook's Journal During His First Voyage Round the World Made in H.M. Bark 'Endeavour' 1769–71," n.d., <http://www.gutenberg.org/files/8106/8106-h/8106-h.htm> (February 2, 2009).

5. William R. Gray, *Voyages to Paradise: Exploring in the Wake of Captain Cook* (Washington, D.C.: The National Geographic Society, 1981), p. 36.

6. Ibid.

7. Hough, p. 42.

8. Ibid., p. 64.

9. Ibid.

10. J. C. Beaglehole, *The Life of Captain James Cook* (Stanford, Calif.: Stanford University Press, 1974), pp. 182–183.

11. John R. Hale, *Age of Exploration* (New York: Time Incorporated, 1974), p. 151.

12. Ibid., p. 152.

13. Ibid.

14. Hough, pp. 140–141.

15. Daniel Conner and Lorraine Miller, *Master Mariner: Capt. James Cook and the Peoples of the Pacific* (Seattle: University of Washington Press, 1978), p. 12.

16. Ibid.

Chapter 4. The Search for the Unknown Continent

1. Nicholas Thomas, *Cook: The Extraordinary Voyages of Captain James Cook* (New York: Walker & Company, 2003), p. 163.

2. Daniel Conner and Lorraine Miller, *Master Mariner: Capt. James Cook and the Peoples of the Pacific* (Seattle: University of Washington Press, 1978), pp. 16–17.

3. James Cook, "A Voyage Towards the South Pole and Round the World," vol. 1, n.d., <http://www.gutenberg.org/files/15777/15777-8.txt> (February 2, 2009).

4. Richard Hough, *Captain James Cook* (New York: W. W. Norton & Company, 1994), p. 235.

5. Cook, "A Voyage Towards the South Pole and Round the World."

6. Thomas, p. 225.

7. Hough, p. 255.

8. James Cook, "A Voyage Towards the South Pole and Round the World," vol. 2, n.d., <http://www.gutenberg.org/files/15869/15869-8.txt> (February 2, 2009).

9. J. C Beaglehole, *The Life of Captain James Cook* (Stanford, Calif.: Stanford University Press, 1974), p. 433.

10. Conner and Miller, p. 19.

Chapter 5. The Fateful Pacific Expedition

1. J. C. Beaglehole, *The Life of Captain James Cook* (Stanford, Calif.: Stanford University Press, 1974), p. 445.

2. Richard Hough, *Captain James Cook* (New York: W. W. Norton & Company, 1994), p. 314.

3. Laurie Lawlor, *Magnificent Voyage: An American Adventurer on Captain James Cook's Final Expedition* (New York: Holiday House, 2002), p. 98.

4. Ibid., p. 113.

5. John R. Hale, *Age of Exploration* (New York: Time Incorporated, 1974), p. 159.

Chapter 6. A Captain's Legacy

1. Tony Horwitz, *Blue Latitudes* (New York: Henry Holt, 2002), p. 79.

2. Ibid., p. 331.

3. Ibid.

4. Richard Hough, *Captain James Cook* (New York: W. W. Norton & Company, 1994), p. 218.

5. Horwitz, pp. 177–178.

Glossary

Aborigines—The first Australians.

Admiralty—The executive department or officers having general authority over British naval affairs.

Antarctic—The South Polar region.

apprentice—A person learning a craft or trade from an employer.

Arctic—The North Polar region.

botanist—A scientist who studies plants.

chronometer—A very accurate clock used as a navigational instrument to determine longitude at sea.

circumnavigation—Going completely around (as the earth), especially by water.

collier—A ship that carries coal.

colonies—Territories settled by people from other countries and controlled by those countries.

coral—Hard, sharp underwater structures made up of the skeletons of millions of tiny creatures.

equator—An imaginary line around the middle of the earth that is drawn on maps.

fauna—The animal life of a particular area.

fjords—Narrow inlets of the sea between cliffs or steep slopes.

flora—The plant life of a particular area.

Great Barrier Reef—A 1,250-mile-long coral reef off the northeast coast of Queensland, Australia.

Great Southern Continent—A large continent believed to exist in the far southern part of the Pacific Ocean, also called *Terra Australis*.

haberdashery—A shop dealing in men's clothing and accessories.

hemisphere—Half of a sphere, especially of the earth.

inlets—Narrow bodies of water that lead inland from larger bodies of water, such as the ocean.

latitude—A distance measured in degrees north or south of the equator.

longboats—Large oared boats usually carried by a merchant ship.

longitude—A distance measured in degrees east or west from a line on the map joining Greenwich, England, and the North and South poles.

master—A person licensed to command a merchant ship.

mate—An officer of a merchant ship, under a captain.

Melanesians—The indigenous peoples of Melanesia, the islands in the Pacific northeast of Australia and south of Micronesia.

navigation—The method of setting the course of a ship.

Northwest Passage—An ice-free water route believed to exist across the top of North America connecting the Atlantic and Pacific oceans.

Polynesians—The indigenous peoples of Polynesia, the islands of the central and southern Pacific.

quadrant—An instrument for measuring vertical angles.

reef—A ridge of coral, rock, or sand near the surface of the sea.

scurvy—A disease caused by not getting vitamin C for a long time.

sextant—An instrument to measure angles, used in navigation.

shoals—Sandbanks or sandbars that make the water shallow.

surveying—The measurement and mapping of parts of the earth's surface.

transit of Venus—When Venus's path takes it directly between the Earth and the Sun.

Further Reading

Books

Beales, R. A. *James Cook: The Pacific Coast and Beyond.* New York: Crabtree Publishing Co., 2006.

Bingham, Jane. *Captain Cook's Pacific Explorations.* Chicago: Heinemann Library, 2008.

Bowen, Richard. *Captain Cook: British Explorer.* Philadelphia: Mason Crest Publishers, 2003.

Broderick, Enid. *Captain James Cook.* Milwaukee, Wis.: World Almanac Library, 2004.

Lawlor, Laurie. *Magnificent Voyage: An American Adventurer on Captain Cook's Final Expedition.* New York: Holiday House, 2002.

Meltzer, Milton. *Captain James Cook: Three Times Around the World.* New York: Benchmark Books, 2002.

Myers, Walter Dean. *Antarctica: Journeys to the South Pole.* New York: Scholastic Press, 2004.

Internet Addresses

Captain Cook Timeline
<http://www.captcook-ne.co.uk/ccne/timeline.htm>

Captain James Cook
<http://library.hanover.edu/cook/>

James Cook and the Transit of Venus
<http://science.nasa.gov/headlines/y2004/28may_cook.htm>

Index

A

Aborigines, 54–56, 100, 102
Adventure, HMS, 62, 69–71, 74. *See also* second voyage.
Antarctic, 65–68, 71–72, 75, 88
Antelope, HMS, 34
Australia, 9–17, 49, 53–57, 61, 97, 99–100, 102

B

Banks, Joseph, 47, 99
  on coral reef stranding, 10, 14, 15
  described, 39
  on equator crossing ceremony, 42, 43
  on fame, 59
  plant collection by, 55
  refusal, on second voyage, 62
Bligh, William, 81
Botany Bay (Stingray Bay), 54, 55
Buchan, Alexander, 39

C

Cape Horn, 44, 72, 75, 80
chronometer, 63–65, 99
Clerke, Charles, 80, 81, 95
Colville, Alexander, 31, 33
Cook, Elizabeth Batts (wife), 31, 34
Cook, James
  birth, 19
  childhood/family life, 19–20
  children, 31, 34, 35
  death, 93
  education, 19–26
  on fame, 59
  as leader, 11–17, 37–38, 48
  legacy, 97–102
  marriage, 31
  military career, 26–31
  motivations, 25
  promotion of, 38, 76
  as surveyor. *See* surveyor duties.

D

Dalrymple, Alexander, 37
Discovery, HMS, 81, 82, 84, 86, 89, 90, 95. *See also* third voyage.
Duc d'Aquitaine, SS, 27
Dutch East India Company, 53

E

Eagle, HMS, 26–27
Easter Island, 71, 72–73, 74
Egmont, Mount (Taranaki, Mount), 52
Endeavor, HMS. *See also* first voyage.
  coral reef stranding, 9–17
  desertion, 48
  equator crossing, 42–44
  preparation of, 38–40
  Tahiti, 40–42, 44–48

F

first voyage. *See also Endeavor,* HMS.
  disease, 57
  motivations, 36–37, 53
  results of, 58–59
  theft issues, 46
Förster, Johann Reinhold, 62
France, 26–28, 37

Freelove, 22–24
French Canada, conquest of, 28–31
Friendly Islands, 69, 82
Friendship, SS, 24–25
Furneaux, Tobias, 62, 65, 68–71, 74, 82

G
Graves, Thomas, 34
Great Barrier Reef (Australia), 9–17, 55, 58, 61
Great Southern Continent *(Terra Australis),* 37, 47, 53–54, 61, 75, 77
Green, Charles, 39, 47, 52
Greenwich Hospital administration, 79
Grenville, HMS, 34–35, 36

H
Hamar, Joseph, 26
Harrison, John, 64–65
Hawaii (Sandwich Islands), 81, 82–84, 88–93

L
Lords of the Admiralty, 27, 33, 35–38

M
Maori
   European effects on, 100–102
   first voyage, 49–51
   second voyage, 68, 71, 73, 74–75
   third voyage, 82
Medway, HMS, 27
Merchant Navy, 22–26
Mercury, transit of, 52

Montcalm, Louis-Joseph de, 30–31

N
Newfoundland, 31, 33–36
New Hebrides, 74
New South Wales, 57
New Zealand, 99, 100
   second voyage, 67–69, 74–75
   survey of, 48–53, 57–58
   third voyage, 82
North America, 84–88
Northumberland, HMS, 31, 33
Northwest Passage, 80, 88, 90, 95

P
Palliser, Hugh, 26–27
Parkinson, Sydney, 39, 54–55
Pembroke, HMS, 27–31
Point Venus, 46
Possession Island, 57

Q
Quebec City, 30–31
Queen Charlotte Sound, 53, 67–71, 74, 82

R
Resolution, HMS, 62, 69–71, 81. *See also* second voyage; third voyage.
Rio de Janeiro, 42
Royal Society, 35–37, 39, 40, 59, 61, 76

S
Sanderson, William, 20–21
sauerkraut, 40–41
scurvy, 28, 41–42, 76
second voyage

accomplishments, 76–77
Antarctic, 65–68, 71–72
departure, 61–63
Easter Island, 72–73
New Hebrides, 74
plan, general, 65
position, determining,
    63–65
Tierra del Fuego, 75
Tonga, 68–69
weather issues, 65–67,
    69, 71–72
Seven Years' War, 26–28
Simcoe, John, 27, 29
Society Islands, 48–49,
    68, 71
Solander, Daniel, 39, 42,
    47, 55, 59
solar eclipse, 35
surveyor duties
    education in, 28–30
    Newfoundland, 33–36
    New Zealand, 48–53,
        57–58
    Tahiti, 47

T
Tahiti
    European effects on,
        99–100
    first voyage, 40–42,
        44–48
    second voyage, 68, 73
    survey of, 47
    third voyage, 82
Tasman, Abel, 48, 53–54
Tasmania, 49, 82
tattooing, 51
third voyage
    Cook as commander of,
        79–80
    Hawaii, 82–84, 88–93

motivations for, 80–81
North America, 84–88
route, general, 81–82
Tasmania, 82
Three Brothers, SS, 24
Tierra del Fuego,
    42–44, 75
Tonga, 68–69
Tweed, HMS, 34

V
Vancouver, George, 81
Venus, transit of, 36, 40,
    44–47

W
Walker, John, 22, 24–26,
    59, 63, 79
Wharton, William, 35–36
Wolfe, James, 30–31